THE

MENTOR WITH LYNN

MARKETING SERIES

BOOK 1

CALLING ALL LEADS

THE 10 MINUTE PHONE INTERVIEW

BY

Lynn Leach

Calling All Leads is designed to help overcome the fear of the phone and prepare you for success in implementing the telephone to grow your business. The 10 minute phone interview script is designed to help position you as the professional, make the sorting and sifting process painless and identify those hot prospects. This is the

first in a series of marketing training for network marketers.

PLEASE REVIEW THIS BOOK ON AMAZON.COM.

It will help me make the next version better. I appreciate your input.

Peace, Health and Prosperity.

ABOUT THE AUTHOR

Lynn Leach has been
involved with the industry
of MLM/network
marketing and direct
sales for 45 years. She is
a retired Pastor (as
retired as any Pastor can
be!), and owns Common
Scents Health Research
and Wellness Centers and
Leach Publishing. You can
reach Lynn at 724-292-

8481 or email her at
pastorlynn@comcast.net
and her wellness center
website is
www.LynnLeach.com

Her corporate website
with Paid2Save is:
www.Paid2Save.com/past
orlynn

and her Viral Card is:
http://viralcard.paid2save.
com/72454

Her training site is
www.mentorwithlynn.com

PREPARING YOURSELF

Are you having success with calling a lead list? I know that when I had to start calling leads, I was terrified. I had no idea how to work them. I literally shook as I picked up the phone; beads of perspiration dropped from my forehead and I stumbled over every word – I was PATHETIC!

I had actually never had to use the phone to cold call leads until 1991. I had been in sales with Tupperware and Celebrity Jewelry, but had always booked shows from shows to keep my business flowing. I joined Mary Kay Cosmetics primarily for tax purposes, and (of course) just to get my make up at a discount. But after taking a leave of absence from corporate restaurant management due to cancer, I soon discovered that I had really not had a life in that field. It was very demanding and required long hours. So I decided to work the Mary Kay. Funds were very low for us at that time due to medical bills. I went to my director and told her that I needed to work this. She said I could buy a share in a bridal show that was taking place the next day. It was $60.00 for 1/24th of the show. I know this sounds bad...but I did not have $60.00. But I took $60.00 from the grocery money, and I bought a share. Three days later I went to her house and she handed me a stack of little slips of paper. Those were my leads. I looked at her with a puzzled expression on my face and asked, "What do I do with these?" And she said, "You call them and book a show with them." I told her I did not know how to do that. She just said that it was easy and handed me a paper with a script on it. I am not sure exactly what I had expected I had purchased...but I certainly had not expected I would have to call anyone. I guess I just wasn't thinking. I crumpled the script and stuck it in my pocket.

I left and my stomach was churning all the way home. I had to get the $60.00 back for groceries or my 3 boys would not eat! When I got home, my husband and the boys were in the living room watching TV. So I took the leads and went upstairs to my bedroom. I sat on the bed and pulled the phone over. I pulled the crumpled script out and smoothed it out so I could read it. Now I am not kidding here when I say I was terrified. I was shaking, my stomach was upset and beads of perspiration were literally dropping from my forehead onto the slips of paper. I picked up the receiver and I dialed the first number. When the lady answered, I somehow blurted out the words on the paper, stumbling and stuttering over each word. When I got to the last sentence and asked if she would like to book a facial, she answered "YES!" I was so shocked I said, "Really? Thank you," And then I hung up!!! I had not even asked for the date and time! A minute after I hung up, I had to call her back and ask for the date. She must have thought I was stone cold crazy! I am not sure what would have happened if she had said no. I made another call and got another yes. I called 15 out of 22 leads and got 11 bookings over the next 3 days! I made over $5,000.00 in 2 months from those shows, and went on target to win my first car with Mary Kay and to become a director. And that first lady – well, she signed up as one of my first recruits and went on to help me win that car. I am just glad I took the action to pick up the phone in the first place...but I had actually cornered myself and was in a position where I had to make it work. DESIRE was definitely there, but looking back, I see how comical it all was. But when I was going through it...that fear of the phone was extremely real.

I wish I had a video of that night. But I soon turned a very weak area (in fact, my weakest) into a strong skill. Here is the key: Talents, you are born with – Skills, you acquire. You can learn any skill. So have an open mind, be willing to learn new skills and then take action. Do not let the fear stop you.

Do you remember the first time your tried to ride a bike? How about the first time you tried to roller skate or ice skate? And how did you feel the first time you got behind the wheel of a car? And who can forget that first day of a new job. Scary isn't it? Well, the phone is similar. It's hard the first time. The second and third time is still uncomfortable. But the more you do it...the easier it gets.

Get a good script to use in the beginning. Practice

the script at least 2 dozen times **BEFORE** you get on the phone. Practice it in front of a mirror. Now I know that sounds silly, but it works – it reminds you to **SMILE**. The more you practice, the easier it is for the words to roll off of your tongue. Pretty soon you will be able to say the words in your sleep – **BACKWARDS!!!** I cannot stress enough how

important it is to practice, practice, practice.

10 MINUTE PHONE INTERVIEW

What if I could show you a way to easily get the attention of people you are cold calling from a lead list of business opportunity seekers? In network marketing, people sometimes come off desperate. They get nervous and tend to throw up their opportunity all over people. They get excited about their opportunity and simply give out too much information too soon.

Think about this: If someone were to go and apply for a position with any company, what would they have to do? Fill out an application and go through an interview. One of the big perks of owning your own business and building your own team with networking marketing companies is that you actually get to pick and choose who you want to work with. You want workers on your team. You want disciplined people who will be committed to consistently work a set number of hours per week. You need to treat this like a business – YOUR business. So you want to be a little selective about who you place on your team. It is a mindset.

I have a script that we have had wonderful success with in conjunction with the 10 minute phone interview. It works well with teams of 2. One person calls and sets up the appointment, and one person does the interview. Makes it all look so very professional. Make it a goal to share your opportunity with someone local so you have an accountability partner and someone to work with. Have fun with it. I work closely with my best friend, Irene Baker. We genuinely have tons of fun working our business, whether it is cold calling, working a table event or attending network marketing events. You can also do both the booking and the interview yourself. I have put both forms of the booking script in the next chapter for you.

Here is the important thing. Every word in the booking script is there for a reason. Please use the script exactly the way it is. Do not deviate from this one. Get all of the words out quickly -- do not even take a breath between sentences. Have the attitude and belief that of course they want to do the interview. You need to remove all negativity from your mind.

With the interview script, you will need to have someone who can listen, process information quickly and respond appropriately. Each interview will be different, depending on the answers to the questions you ask. The questions are designed to get them talking. You will need to listen so you can key in on the hot button for the personality you are speaking with so you can move to close the sale. It is VERY important to understand that you need to listen -- and listen carefully. God gave you 2 ears and only one mouth. So take a lesson from that -- you need to listen twice as much as you talk. Take notes on everything you glean from the interview.

If you sign the prospect, you will want to make sure you remember everything about them so you can begin to build that relationship that is so important. After all, this is a relationship building business.

Once the appointment is set up, and you are actually in the middle of conducting it, you will find that the prospects will open up and begin to sell themselves to you...just as if they were sitting in a live interview. Now this will require you to study all of the chapters in this book, and implement all of the information that is presented. It all fits together to make this marketing strategy work.

Please remember to set your follow up appointment with them. The fortune is in the follow up and you need to schedule a time when they will review your information and a time for you to connect with them immediately following their review. If you fail to follow up -- you will not make the sale or sign the recruit. It is that simple. You will leave money on the table. Yes, you may get a few here and there that will call you...but the majority will forget to call you and then the opportunity has left their mind as they get busy with everyday life and attending to their priorities. You need to control the situation, and schedule the appointment, make the call and close the sale.

There is a psychology to sales and these scripts are no different. They are easy to learn, but please take heed and practice with them so that you are comfortable with them. Practice until you sound natural and not like you are reading from a script. Practice until the words flow off your tongue smoothly. Practice until the script is imbedded in your brain and becomes a part of you. The key to making this script work is that you come off as a professional. And as a

**small business owner --
you ARE a professional.**

YOUR LEAD LIST

You can purchase a lead list from a reputable vendor – always check with your up-line to see what they are using. But, it is better to generate the leads yourself. There are hundreds of ways to do that, and I have training on many of those ways.

I also need to let you know that you need to distinguish between a lead, a prospect and a red hot prospect. Leads need to be sorted and sifted. When I generate my leads, I send them to my sizzle line. I have specific training in other books in this series on the sizzle line set up, scripting, and how to get people to go to that sizzle line. The sizzle line automatically sorts and sifts my leads for me so that now I only have to call actual prospects who are genuinely interested in my product or my opportunity. SOOOO MUCH EASIER!!! Please refer to the sizzle line books in the MENTOR WITH LYNN MARKETING SERIES.

SCRIPTS

You will want to practice these scripts before you begin to call. Use the scripts until you feel comfortable and confident. You will eventually be able to do your calls without the script, and you will find your personality coming through on all of your calls.

BOOKING SCRIPT:

Hi _____. My name is
_____ and I am calling
to see if we could
schedule a 5 to 10 minute
phone interview with you
to see if you would be a
good fit for our
company...we understand
you were looking for a
way to generate an extra
stream of income by
working a side project

from home. Do you have time to do that now?

OR:

Hi _____. My name is _____and I am calling from the office of _____. _____ wanted me to see if we could schedule a 5 to 10 minute phone interview with you to see if you would be a good fit for our company...we understand that you were looking for a way to generate an extra stream of income by working a side project from home. Do you have a few minutes to talk with _____?

INTERVIEW SCRIPT:

Hi _____, how are you today? Great! I am going to ask you a few questions that will help me determine if you are a good fit for our company, and if so, then I am going to give you some information so you can take a look at our company to see if it will be a good fit for you, does that sound fair?

Wonderful! _____, the first question is how many hours per week would you be able to put into a side project working from home?

Okay, ____ how much money are you looking to generate on a monthly basis by working a side project from home?

Alright, _____would you consider yourself to be

people oriented person or a task oriented person?

Great! What are your work preferences? Do you prefer to work on the phone, face to face, on the computer or communicating through mailings?

_____, Can you tell me a little about yourself? Can you tell me what skills you have acquired with your work history...are you working now?

_____, do you consider yourself to be a disciplined person?

Okay, are you a self-starter or do you prefer to have constant direction and supervision?

_____, have you ever worked from home before?

Have you ever owned your own business?

Does the idea of owning your own business, being your own boss and making your own schedule have an appeal to you?

Well, _____ with our company, you would be set up to own your own business, and with having your own business, there is always a cost, right? So there is a little cost to getting set up with us...would that be a problem for you?

Well, _____, I think you would be a good fit for our company and definitely an asset to my team, so now we need to see now if our company would be a good fit for you. We are in the _____industry. Does that hold any appeal for you?

Do you have a computer at home and internet access?

(If so) I would like to get you set up to take a look at our company, the management team, the co-founders, the product,

the way we pay....could
you view a 30 minute
webinar that would give
you a good overview so
you have the information
you need to make an
informed, intelligent
decision as to whether
our company would be a
good fit for you?
At this point you get them
set up with a recorded
webinar, a live webinar or
send them information to
look over, or if you are

working 2x2 as a team....you hand the phone back over to your partner and have your partner set up getting them the information to look at. You then schedule a time when you can call them back to do follow up and close the sale. Try to get a firm time when they will be able to review your information, and then schedule your follow up call 15 minutes after that time. Also, it is advantageous for you to try to get them to review the material immediately following their interview if you can. Life gets busy, and it is easy for them to get caught up in other things and forget to review your information. So get this scheduled in as quickly as possible.

(If no computer) I would like to send you some information for you to review. (Send them your printed information, CD or DVD.)

IDENTIFY THE HOT BUTTON

I use a modified version of the DISC System to hone in on personality types quickly so I can identify the hot button for closing the sale. So I am just going to give you some basic keys to look for. I highly recommend you go and take a course in the DISC System...but this will

give you enough
information to begin with.

First of all, there is no
right or wrong personality
type. Each type has
strengths and
weaknesses. The
importance of recognizing
the differences is to help
you understand how to
work with different
people, and specifically
for our purposes here, to
quickly identify the hot

button of the prospect
you are speaking with.
THERE ARE 4 MAJOR
TYPES:
D = DOMINATE
I = INFLUENCING
S = STEADY
C = COMPLIANT

DOMINANCE

This is with respect to control, power and assertiveness. This personality is very active in dealing with problems and challenges. High "D" people are described as demanding, forceful, egocentric, strong willed, driving, determined, ambitious, aggressive, and pioneering. They have some effective traits: they can be very direct, very

self-assured, they get
results and they are the
take charge personality.
Their ineffective traits
can make them appear as
being dictatorial,
demanding, and sarcastic.
You can identify this
personality type by asking
them to tell you a little bit
about themselves. They
will list off all of their
achievements, titles,
education and degrees,
awards they have won,

positions they hold, etc. It is all about them...they need to have the attention and demand respect. To close this personality type, key in on advancing quickly and leadership roles with titles -- those are important to them. They can make a snap decision if they can see a future in leadership for themselves, and you can close them with 1 appointment.

INFLUENCE

This is relating to social situations and communication. The High "I" influences others through talking and activity and tends to be very emotional. They are described as convincing, magnetic, political, enthusiastic, persuasive, warm, demonstrative, trusting, and optimistic. Their effective traits include being people oriented, persuasive, caring, and motivational. Their ineffective traits cause them to talk too much and they lack focus. You can identify an "I" easily because they will talk a lot – they are very social. They are the life of the party, the fun, bubbly personality that everyone enjoys being around. To close an "I" you focus in on the fun stuff -- they are motivated by prizes and recognition. They can make a snap decision and don't need to know any details -- and usually don't bother to find any of the details out later either, as they simply don't care about them. You can close them in one appointment.

STEADINESS

This is relating to patience, persistence, and thoughtfulness. The High "S" wants a steady pace, security, and does not like sudden change. An "S" personality is calm, relaxed, patient, possessive, predictable, deliberate, stable, consistent, and tends to be unemotional about the business opportunity and they are the ones with a poker face. Their effective traits make them a good listener, and they are loyal and consistent. Their ineffective traits are: indecisive and resistant to change. You can identify the "S" personality by asking them to tell you a little about themselves. Because they are the family oriented person, they will talk about their family instead of themselves. They will talk about what their spouse has done in the way of achievements, and what their children have accomplished. It is all about the family. To close an "S", remember that they are motivated by the fact that this fits by allowing them to place their family as a higher priority than work. Talk about the stability of your company, as that will be important to them. It will usually take more than one appointment to close them.

COMPLIANT

This is relating to structure and organization (conscientious). The High "C" adheres to rules, regulations, and structure. They like to do quality work and do it right the first time. They can be described as careful, cautious, exacting, neat, systematic, diplomatic, accurate, and tactful.

Their effective traits
make them accurate and
they are detailed
oriented. Their ineffective
traits are: they can be
critical, accurate, and
perfectionistic. Now you
might wonder why being a
perfectionist would be an
ineffective trait, but in
this instance it is because
they will get bogged down
by the details or want
everything to be so
perfect that when it is

not, they become paralyzed. You can always identify the "C" because they will ask a lot of questions. They will want details about everything. They are the ones who read all of the Policies and Procedures, the Terms and Conditions, and all fine print...even if they have to get a magnifying glass. To close a "C", you must realize that this is the detailed oriented person who has to know all of the details about everything. They cannot make a decision quickly because they have to research all the details. It will take two, three or more appointments to close them.

The questions in the interview are designed to help you key in on the hot

button so you can proceed to close the sale.

CLOSE THE SALE

After they have had an opportunity to review your company information by attending a live or recorded webinar, going on a live or recorded conference call, reviewing or touring your website or viewing a DVD or listening to a CD, you need to follow up with them. The follow up call is where you will get their response to your information and ask if they have any questions. This is where you would address any objections and calm any fears they have about whether they would be able to learn how to do the business. I would refer you to my material on the POA (Plan Of Action). Understanding that material will help you move their belief in their ability to fit the business into their lifestyle comfortably.

After addressing any questions they have, and alleviating any fears they might bring up, you must move to ask for the sale. This is where many people fumble because they are not comfortable with it. Figure out your closing spiel and practice it until it becomes a vital part of you. Here is mine:

"Sounds like this would be a perfect fit for you and I know you are a good fit for the team. I'm really looking forward to working with you. Let's get you set up so we can begin your training. Would you like to start with the Business Builder Pack, or is the Starter Pack more what you had in mind?" Then I shut up. Give them a choice between something and something, never give them an opportunity to select between yes or no. Take your 2 highest priced starter packs and give them a choice. You make the offer... and then you do not speak again. You just keep dead silent until they respond. They will let you know where they are at. If the cost is an issue, they will let you know, and then you just take it down until you find their comfort level.

The issue is YOU MUST ASK FOR THE SALE. If you have conducted your interview in such a way as to help you identify the hot button, and then keyed in on that hot button, you should have no problem in closing the sale.

With practice and experience, you will find

that your closing ratio will improve. In the beginning you may close 1 in 10, but as you continue to work this you will sharpen your skills and you will find you are signing 2 out of 10, and then 3 out of 10. It is a numbers game, and monitoring your closing ratio is part of tracking and evaluating your progress. Practice and then work it.

Just remember that the sale of a product is simply finding the need and showing how your product fills the need. Recruiting is the same – find the need and show how your opportunity will fill the need. If you key in on the NEED – or HOT BUTTON -- you WILL close!

READY, SET, GO

Setting your intentions and your mindset are so very important to your success in developing your phone skills.

Let's talk a little about your mindset first. You MUST have belief in your business. That means you must be a product of the product you are trying to sell. You must have a belief in the product, the company, the owners, the management team, the comp plan, and the opportunity you are promoting. This is key to your success. If you do not believe in what you are offering, it will come across to your prospects as you speak with them. They will hear it in your voice. When you have belief in your opportunity and product, they hear that in your voice. They will catch your enthusiasm.

You need to have a core belief that, of course this person will benefit from my opportunity or product. Of course they will be interested in what I have to say. They will naturally want to join me. In fact having that core belief is so important, that I recommend you write out affirmations about it and speak those affirmations out loud daily until you believe it with every fiber of your being.

Now I want to address your perspective on the sorting and sifting process of cold calling a lead list. Some might pick the phone up and call for 10 minutes and get discouraged and quit, thinking this is not for them. Again I tell you -- THIS IS A NUMBERS GAME. The sorting and sifting does pay off, if you can discipline yourself to put the time in to learn a system, get comfortable with it and then have fun while you work it.

Do you remember the gold rush? Everyone was so excited to go panning for gold. Well calling a lead list is like panning for gold. You are sorting and sifting for the gold nuggets. Takes a lot of time and patience...but when you find a gold nugget -- WOW!!! Cold calling is sorting and sifting -- you are looking for the gold nuggets -- those customers who will buy your product, or sign up as a brand partner on your team. They are precious, and very valuable.

To justify the time you will invest in the sorting and sifting process, I suggest you work your figures. You need to know the CLV, or customer lifetime value of someone who becomes a customer or signs up as a team member. Once you have that figured, then you can work out your ROI or return of investment for your time and marketing dollars you spend on your lead list. You will soon discover that this is well worth your time even in the beginning when your closing ratio is low. And of course as your closing ratio improves...look out!

Okay, now it is time to set your intention. This is so important and one thing that many people overlook. You must set your intention. Write your intentions out. Make a chart of what you intend to do. Now please remember to keep it realistic. Set your intentions in front of you.

Speak them out loud. Believe in your heart -- actually PURPOSE IN YOUR HEART – that, you will achieve the intentions you set. I will tell you this: it is 90% intention and 10% skill. NO joke. Try it...you will see.

When you are ready to make your first call, please DRESS THE PART. Put on your Sunday best. Again, I know it sounds silly, but just think about it. Don't you feel your best when you are all dressed up? Your attitude will come over the phone lines...you need to look and feel your best. So get dressed up, fix your hair; ladies - put on your make-up; gentlemen – shave, put on your fragrance. You will **FEEL THE PART OF A PROFFESSIONAL.** Now set a mirror in front of you. SET YOUR INTENTION, and take action – remember: there can be no results if you never take action. So...

SMILE...

Wink at yourself...

And repeat these words. "YOU HOT DOG!"

Now, PICK UP THE PHONE

Lynn's other books:

__NEW RULES FOR SUCCESS__ **with John Spencer Ellis**

__DARE TO SUCCEED__ **with Jack Canfield**

__AGAINST THE GRAIN__ **with Brian Tracy**

__SUCCESSONOMICS__ **with Steve Forbes**

The WILDERNESS VOYAGE Devotional Series:

__BOOK 1: REBELLION__

__BOOK 2: MANIPULATION__

__BOOK 3: DEPRESSION__

BOOK 4: FORGIVENESS

BOOK 5: REJECTION

BOOK 6: BITTER ROOTS

BOOK 7: PRIDE

BOOK 8: GREED

The MENTOR WITH LYNN Marketing Series:

BOOK 1: CALLING ALL LEADS

BOOK 2: SIZZLE YOUR WAY TO SUCCESS

BOOK 3: DROP YOUR SIZZLE

BOOK 4: SIZZLE SIGNS